Under the Mistletoe of Dreams

Under
The Mistletoe
Of
Dreams

POEMS

J. R. PHILLIPS

Illumina Press
Pasadena, California

Copyright © 2017 by J. R. Phillips

All rights reserved. No part of this book may be used or reproduced in any manner whatsoever without written permission, except in the case of brief quotations embodied in critical articles or reviews.

Art work and design by author.
Typography by author.
Photography by author.

ISBN: 978-0-9986160-8-7

Printed by Illumina Press
in the United States of America

http://www.illuminapress.org

CONTENTS

Preface	9
Under the Mistletoe of Dreams	11
For Fiona, Christmas Eve 2009	13
I	15
Prelude to this Yule	17
Under The Mistletoe Of Dreams	19
O All The Chimneys In The Christmas Towns	21
A Predication of Snow	22
Vespers	24
He Walks Among Fireflies	25
Winter Chimes	27
A Carriage in Central Park	28
In a Monastery Garden	30
New Years Eve	32
Newgrange	34
Everyman Ascending	36
An Exaltation of Larks	37
A Sacrament of Love	38
Annunciation	40
Into the Light	43

When the Summer Dies	44
Air (Orchestral Suite)	45
II	49
Visions & Apparitions	51
Sestina: Beata Mea Domina	69
III	73
Madrigals & Motets	75
Introduction	77
Tears that stain the sight of vision	79
I love you without reason or prayer	80
Late in the day	81
Beauty runs rich in your deep brown bewildered eyes	82
Of your amorous ways	84
Lilacs in the morning	86
We breathe flowers, you and I	88
O the stain won't come off	90
There are lots of bright flowers	91
I have known many women	92
IV	93
Two Christmas Ballads for Keyboard & Guitar	95
Christmas Lullaby	99
Winter Solstice	101

for FIONA

*Under the mistletoe of dreams, a star—
As though to join us at some distant hill—
Turns in the waking west and goes to sleep.*

—Hart Crane

Preface

Much of this book is comprised of selections from previous works published many years back. I have always felt the holiday seasons merited a special occasion for a celebration of poetry and music. Certainly judging by the popularity of Christmas carols, the sacred music of Handel and Bach, the tales of Dickens and Dylan Thomas—such sentiment seems equally shared by a myriad of revelers besides myself. So it is with this spirit of holiday cheer and Yuletide observation, I dedicate this little book of lyric poetry and the accompanied Compact Disk which includes two musical compositions arranged by the accomplished jazz musician Herman Jackson.

Under the Mistletoe of Dreams

For Fiona, Christmas Eve 2009

Tomorrow
When all dreams become possibilities,
I see you there in the garden on the hill
Near the ocean,
The sky bright blue, the white wispy clouds,
The cool fragrant air.
I see you there, a Renoir canvas,
More beautiful than a painter's perfect rendering.
There where the sun-glistened grass
Combs a trail of emeralds along your floating feet,
I see you like some gypsy maiden in a Rabbie Burns ballad.
I see you there Sylvan and simple,
Twisting a poppy stem or gathering pebbles
From the California shore.
The sun silhouettes your frame,
Colors more vibrant and varied surround you.
That lone stone cottage by the murmuring sea,
Those warm winter evenings by the flickering fire
And you beside me beneath a blanket or quilt...
These visions I treasure and nourish
As a fine wine or a rare gemstone.
You beside me by the fire or in my arms,
You beside me in my arms and in my heart
In the cottage by the sea
Where all dreams become possibilities.

Prelude To This Yule

Here we are again.

The inculcating stars are predictably aligned

As another winter solstice unfolds before our eyes.

Department store windows will display their frosted trim,

The streets will fill with shoppers and workers

Laying on their horns,

Queuing down the boulevards of lights,

While merchants pray for a prosperous deliverance

And economists keep tally of the daily grind.

Meanwhile back at the world

The trees dip their branches in the new fallen snow,

Rivers run to ice, and only

The swishing sounds of a distant skier

Disturbs the sacred silence that blankets the land.

The land, at last, gets a breather

From the follies of earth's feeble-footed brood.

The cold has a cleansing effect on human nature,

Forcing a temporary truce
On our binge-and-purge demeanor.

Here we are again
Facing another fading year with ringing bells
And singing cash registers
While the world teeters on the edge
And the balance between us
Is more fragile than ever.

Under The Mistletoe Of Dreams

The night's air breathes a gesture of stars

Upon the moon-lit skyline.

The hilltops are tipped with new fallen snow.

The cities of the world drape themselves

In raiments of gold-spangled garlands

And the children rush to bed without prodding,

Anxious for the morning treasure,

Dreaming what magic their little minds can muster.

And we dream too, for a little,

Dream of the distant stars

And childhood's first glimpse

At the purity of snowfall,

Dream of the pine-scented hills and the singing wind,

Dream and remember the youth of our years,

The simple joys and the extravagance of nature.

You turn from the window

And move to join me by the fire.

We stare into the crackling flames

And remember all the Christmases

That have come and gone

Before and beyond our middle-age years.

Here beneath this canopy of stars,

Beneath this mistletoe of dreams,

We stand firm against the tides that turn our hearts

And harden us to the wonders of the world.

Under the mistletoe of dreams,

A holly-wreath of stars,

Our fingers forge a kiss in the dark

As our lips make a vow never to stray our hearts.

O All The Chimneys In The Christmas Towns

O all the chimneys in the Christmas towns,
The thick blue smoke from the little brick houses,
And the moon-glowing snow and the snow-thick roofs
And the chapel steeples and the bright blue lakes,
Shine in the store front windows
And the greeting-card covers on the fireplace mantel
And in all the eyes of infants
And angels that are dreamed of
In the green holly hills and the pine-sweet skies.

O all the chimneys in the star-steepled night
And the icy windows and the caroling choirs,
Though children go hungry
And the world grow weary of all its wars,
Come, Christmas dreams of evergreen air
And the little winter cottage with the corner fire,
Ring a jingle-bell joy to all that's left to love
In this war-weary world and be warm.

A Predication of Snow

Winter's white sky, turn of the solstice,
By the stony lake and for no man's eyes but these:
This hallowed hill, this silent music.
The sun moves southward, sifting light
As it falls through the thick icy air.
Only the brightness of snow and the white snowy clouds
Shrouding the dead moon contain the moment.
Only this life-bleeding ground
And the shadow of rocks and trees along the lake
Contain what is worth recalling,
Contain what is worth invoking
On this cold silent night
In the hills above the city.
For the city bears no particular parlance
That could utter a truth nor alter the eye.
Its language is shrill and monotonous,
Its image cluttered and dull as the human mind.

Only here on this ground, by this lake,

At this waning of the winter sun,

Is there comfort from the chaos,

Dominion over the dominating dark.

Only here in this clean, blanched silence,

This white shining stillness

Is the passing of the year given meaning and depth,

Deft in its self-contained brilliance.

No incense nor twelve lit candles add credence

To the sanctity of this spell.

No sullen glow nor sadden séance

Can wrench from this sight

The self-contained purity of this sunless world.

And somewhere beyond the narrow vistas of nations,

Beyond the glare of gold and the flow

Of the bleeding rivers,

A child, in its infinite infancy,

Waits to be born.

Vespers

O peace of night settle gently

On this weary world.

Put all conflict to rest,

Dissonance to dust.

Let stars open and shine

In the dark distant skies.

Sing praise to the mountains,

The ocean, rivers, and streams.

Make bird-song your melody,

The crickets chirp a pillow of sleep.

O slow descending darkness of eve,

Comfort our sleep,

Cradle our dreams in your soft silken skies.

He Walks Among Fireflies

> *The archbishop is away. The church is gray.*
> *He has left his robes folded in camphor*
> *And dressed in black, he walks*
> *Among fireflies.*
>   –Wallace Stevens

The bishop is away.

The sanctity of sun and stars

Lose their shimmer.

With him sails the sea,

The sea with its singing

And its song.

Fireflies flee the night,

Insects mistaken as angels

No longer sparkle in the trees.

The alchemy of evening

Pales against a pallid moon,

A blackened sky.

The yellow sun is deathly

With its ball of fire.

The bells in the village tower

Grow silent and die.

Winter Chimes

A long arduous day

Climbing the cliffs of the Pacific Coast—

The four of us, youthful companions

From puberty to college classrooms,

Sacked out on the hardwood floor,

The smell of coffee from the kitchen stove

And the tinkling chimes on the front-door porch.

The cool soothing wind of winter,

Two hundred miles north of Los Angeles,

Sweeps across these miles of memory

To settle softly and slowly on the leaves of pages

That constitute the changing chapters

Of one man's written life.

Carriage In Central Park

The diamond skies of New York City
Light the eyes of the world and star the night.
The lamplight glows on the icy lake
And the autumn trees and the narrow pathways
That guide the carriage through the dark.
The sounds of taxis and piano bars
Grow fainter and fade with the distance.
We huddle beneath the thick wool blanket
And let the warmth of our bodies
Break the chill of the evening air.
The driver with the crooked hat
Tugs loosely at the reigns—a castoff nobleman
From a black-and-white world.
The steam from our breaths and the horse's nostrils
Trails the path of our journey and blends
With the fog and mist that hover over our heads
Like a watchful angel.

The sights and sounds of moon-dipped Manhattan
Are mythologized like a Cole Porter lyric.
We tip our glasses to toast the town and its magic,
The foam of champagne spills from our hands
And scatters to the sky.
The click-clack click-clack hooves of horses
Pepper the pavement and echo in the distance
Through the years and changing seasons,
Through the dead and dying vestiges of night.

In A Monastery Garden

A lone bell tower breaks
The morning stillness
And calls the world to prayer.

The trees sing a language of bird-song
In counterpoint hymns and chirping sonatas,
The hollyhocks lift their blossoms
To the illuminating skies.
The breath of rosemary and lavender
Lines the narrow walkway.

A sacred solitude blankets
The morning's music.

A lone bell tower
Blesses the trees, the birds,
The flowers

And holds communion over

These sanctuary rites.

New Years Eve

The noisy little city

Rattles its mad delirium of sound.

Multitudes of relatives and friendly relations

Gather around the midnight's striking hour,

Ringing in the renaissance of years,

Walking in reverse

To the repetitious rhythms of a song.

We sit at the table in solitude and quiet.

We are safe;

Shut in from the chaos and crowds.

The food is good,

The wine warm in the blood of our bodies.

The moment is infinite.

We giggle and play childish games,

Stumble naked to the floor, heavy with drink,

Drunk with delicious desire.

The moment is infinite,

Impervious to the uncertainties of change,

To the pain and sorrow that will rearrange our lives.

Newgrange

For Neil McCarthy

The ancients in Ireland built a dome to commemorate
the circling sun and the dying of the northern light.
I could not help but think back to those who stood before you:
descendants of Ó Loingsigh anglicized to Lynch, my mother's tribe
before the Age of Copper, the Age of Bronze.

The mammoth boulders of Stonehenge
and the great pyramids of Giza
pale in the presence of this immense opening eye.
At "The Bend of the Boyne" they mark you,
the river that bends and turns beneath your sun-lit stare.

The advent of the winter sun will illuminate your sight
where a Celtic Chieftain might kneel down beside you
centuries past to worship the shimmering stone

at the throne of the coming solstice

and the intense glow of the evening stars.

Everyman Ascending

Redeem the habitat that you hover in,
Raise raise the tower to the moon.

Forgive the foibles that follow you,
That curse your hopeful eyes.
Raise raise the tower to the moon.

Forget, for a moment,
All those new-born necessities and vows.
Raise raise the tower to the moon.

Hear the cantata that whispers in your ear,
Feel the flesh of the marble and the stone,
Raise raise the tower to the moon

An Exultation of Larks

The music spins around the cerebral brain
That circles the auditory nerves
To sooth or waken the weary worker
From his obligatory day,

When our mornings become something more
Than a kettle's whistle
And our days to escape the jackhammer's rattle,

When the man at the turnstile turns away,
Ascending the open air,

A gush of geese gather above his head,
An exultation of larks is heard
Heralding the Heavenly Host.

A Sacrament of Love

But no longer at ease here, in the old dispensation,
With an alien people clutching their gods.
                              -T.S. Eliot

Whether we ever learn the truth of that night

Or be resolved in taking comfort in the spirit of the myth,

I am here to tell you it doesn't really matter.

It doesn't really matter whether a man of flesh or a man of spirit

Or no real man at all came to us that night.

What was visited upon the earth was a sacrament of love.

Krishna in his chariot atop the battlefield

As mercenary and counsel to the savagery of war

Or Mohammed, the assassin, the vengeful warrior

At the gates of Mecca proclaiming jihad

Or Buddha withdrawn, impervious to the ways of the world:

None of these, none of these serve to sooth

The anguish and suffering, the sorrow and the hurt.

That lone dark night in the desert,

That dazzling bright star in the evening sky…

We come to you year after year to remember and remind us:

A new commandment I give unto you,

That ye shall love one another; As I have loved you,

Ye also shall love one another.

Annunciation

And the angel answered and said unto her
The Holy Ghost shall come upon thee,
And the power of the Highest shall overshadow thee:
Therefore also that holy thing which shall be born of thee
Shall be called the Son of God
                           Luke 1:35

I

She had a vision that night

something good and gainful

had ripened inside her.

Love came to her darkly

in the form of an angel

—all those years pretending

a devotion to denial

was some sort of virtue.

II

Bleeding and budding

with knowledge

a virgin clasps

an open wound

is made mortal

by passion.

Just as Eve

her sister

alone in the garden

with only God the serpent

disguised as the devil,

his lips and tongue

as sweet as the skin of an apple.

III

She thinks to herself:
My soul, if there is one,
seems thread-bare, inadequate,
and insensate.
My body I know by sense and desire.
It is the vessel I feed
that I nurture and treasure
though the world would have me empty
and chaste, devoid of nature.

I consecrate my heart,
I worship and revere my womanhood,
I welcome the seed bursting
and blooming inside me.

I welcome the flower
that will further my future.

Into The Light

In caves of cathedrals the Clergy casts it spell
On eyes once known for seeing that hover in the dark

The tide of times sweep over the eyes
And covers the doubtful vision with sleep

And no one dare journey beyond the dream of the sky
Into the depth of the light, the silence

For the hand that closes the eyelids with its prayer
Blocks out the sun and smothers the light of vision

Into the depth of the light, the breadth of the silence,
We wander alone, above and beyond the masses

Into the depth of the light, the breadth of the silence
Where we can never know the nothing

When The Summer Dies

When the summer dies,

and the beaches are empty

and the children return to school,

we go down to the town

buy cheese and bread

and a bottle of wine,

spread a blanket on a lone hillside

above the city

and when we are finally done with each other,

boy's body next to girl's body,

we think to ourselves:

how perfect are these cool free days

of approaching winter.

Air (An Orchestral Suite)

After J.S. Bach

Air

The heavens come down from the sky
And circle the room in an auditory air.
You listen. You stare. Your senses are lit
By a burning fire in your ears.
Wings lift you from your chair.
Trees bend. Music flows and flowers.

You ascend.

Air
From orchestral suite number 3

J. S. Bach (1685-1750)
BWV 1068, Mvmt. 2

Public Domain

VISIONS AND APPARITIONS

Modern man protects himself against seeing his own split state by a system of compartments. Certain areas of outer life and of his own behavior are kept, as it were, in separate drawers and are never confronted with one another.
~Carl G. Jung
Man & His Symbols

VISIONS AND APPARITIONS

A Fugue & Tocata in 7 Movements

Siehe, innerer Mann, dien inneres Madchen,
Dieses errungene aus tausend Naturen,
Noch geiliebte Gesehepf.
 —Rainer Maria Rilke

I

FINDING the way, we are always looking.
That lingering shadow that never finds focus
Evades us and eludes us the way a dog's tail
Or a kitten with his ball of twine.

Something might move outside, among the rushes.
Someone might warn us. Others might look away.
Something profound we sense circles and surrounds us
But we only half-notice

For the memory wanes as age will overtake us.
We must move through the years like our days
Remembering only what time will allow us to ponder,
Only what dreams will remind us to save.

For all that we crave seems singular
And for sale. That which we grasp easy:

The harvest, the home, the time in which we toil
Will eventually consume us.

And soon the days will darken, the days will quicken.
And all that we crave becomes a life with no purpose.
Time becomes a luxury. We hold it to our hearts
And anticipate the days that will free us of the grind.

II

A man might view a woman
Statuesque and gaunt
Drawn to the arc of the dawn.
A woman might see a man
Wide-shouldered and bronze
Secure in a comforting way
Tall and forceful.
What lures us seems right,
Purposeful and sustaining to the race.

But another dimension lies hidden

In the mirror of a semi-conscious self

Neither flesh nor shadow.

It predates our being,

It simmers in the air and the world

That surrounds us.

It repeats itself over and over

In an uncovered cave site, an ancient grave stone,

The scribblings and carvings

Reflected in the glare of a flickering flame.

III

A man views a woman in the mirror

Of the reflected "I", mourns the division,

The incision of the severed knot,

Clings to the memory of a state of mutual grace.

Alien and lost, fevered with forgotten pain,

He wanders through a maze of mist scattered
Like shattered shell, woman-bred, broken by birth,
Forever falling through a bottomless pit, fearing death.

The man views the woman, not a boy the Madonna
Nor the old man pining his lost youth.
It is the division of Self and Sensation he sees.
The cleavage of meaning and purpose.

Out of the ash of a forgotten fire,
A silent music, the face of a woman
Eyes tense, lips taut, heart hungry as a hawk.
A face immense, watchful, smoldering
In the dimmest dawn of a man's unconscious mind.
A fierce ferocious din of doubt
Nips at his nights and darkens his dawns.
Pomp and prayer, Mammon and God
Leave him hollow and quenchless.

He is lost. A sorrow bitter and black

Bludgeons all beliefs, bloodies the heart,
Petrifies all emotions. He is heartless.
A void empties his eyes.

Devils dictate the steps he must follow.
Vermin cover his feet,
And murder fills the sidewalks
With its acrid stinging stench.

He is human. Desperate as a dog in heat.
Desolation dances through his eyes like a demon.
He sleeps. Dreams of a consummating image
Perfect as peace, soothing as music. He listens.

What is silent and still in the waking mind
Finds substance and sound in his visionary sleep.
He rises half-asleep and reaches for a word
To scratch in ink, a pen to put to paper..

A heartache, heavy like stone,

Stirs beneath the weight of his words,

A music foreign and fearful

Grows vivid and clear in his unstopped ears.

The sounds he hears speaks of a faraway place,

A space constant but forgotten:

Emerald lakes glisten

In the glow of a warm September sun,

The Black Swan and the Green Rose

Color the clear and spacious sky,

Eyes stare out of the dark and disappear.

IV

In dreams begin all mythologies.

Our minds see symbols

For all we fear and crave:

Dark moon on dark waters,

An empty room

With threatening shadows,
The mothering Muse
With her lips of fire to kiss
And killing the dark
As we fall feverish and forgetting
Beneath the overpowering crush
Of her all-encompassing might.
Wicked bitch!
With her spells and incantations.
Beautiful flower!
With her fragrant breath
And her petal-like belly...

Sparkle of fire,
Sun-blazing sand blasted into crystal,
Water-smooth, shiny as silk...
The man views the woman
In the mirror of the reflected "I"
Sees the other self hidden beneath the surface,
Sees the other self subtle and scorned,

Vulnerable to hurt and suffering.

V

Sudden as a leopard,
Sudden as a leopard lunging from the sky,
His heart is torn.
His heart is torn and his body ravaged.
His heart is torn and his body ripped and ravaged,
Ripped and ravaged like raw carnage,
Like siphoned silt,
Like heaps of silt on red roaring rivers,
Like rivers of blood and rivers of dark waters,
Rivers of rust and rust-rotting waters,
Waters of rain rotting into nether,
Rotting and rolling and riding into nether,
Rotting and rolling and riding and falling,
Falling and fading and dying into dust.
Everything is dust.

The man is dust.

The spirit in the man is dust.

Only the lady lives.

Only the lady lives, the opposite Self,

The Self outside the self, the other "I"

And the lady is withdrawn,

In a white gown, to contemplation,

In a white gown to contemplation.

And the lady speaks:

The gods men worship are the gods of slaves

Pushed upon them, like dope,

In pages of dogma and guilt-driven obedience.

I am the god of the inner space,

The husband to the bride lacking the flame

Of self-illumination. I am the light,

The spirit of the way, virgin to the rake,

Mistress and whore to the celibate,

Animate in all things observed

Yet nonexistent to the unobserving.

I am a world unto itself,

Existent only in the eyes

Of those who would find me.

I am the Icon of a Forgotten Age.

Singers of an ancient song once worshipped me:

Moira to the Greeks, Beauty to Shelley, Keats

And Swinburne. To the pagan I was the myth,

To the Christian an abstraction.

Goddess to the Poet, I was the fire

That lit the torch to the darkness of Death,

The mystery of that which was hidden.

To the actor I was the Act, the mimesis of experience

Amplified, given Body and Motion.

To the Painter I was the color and the sun,

To the Sculptor the shape and the substance,

To the Composer I was the harmony of sound,

I was the shoes on the feet of the dancer!

VI

He feels at once a part of himself that's hidden
Break loose from its captive self
In recognition of its birth-forgotten energy.
Like a fish out of water it gasps and gulps,
Like a child it clings to a closeness of its motherhood.

From the outer regions of forgetfulness
Her face comes nearer, growing keen and clearer
As she perpetuates the stars.
The sense of something lost returned to him
Takes hold of him—hands, ears, eyes,

With the force of her light-emitting stare
Illuminates the night, describes and defines
All vicissitudes of mind, line, and matter.
Angels break from the sky, one by one the muses sing
And all the dark shadows are vanquished from the night.

She seems a thing quite free from him
Yet he knows her face as surely as his own
When, deep in sleep, the Eye turns inward its gaze
And the Mind seeks out a place
From which all memory seems to center.

He knows too the eyes, the look,
The weariness softened to a simmering shine,
The cool blue glow of sadness
Like brook water tremulous, unending.
He thinks of Saint Francis, the agony of Sebastian.

He thinks of Augustine, St. Thomas Aquinas,
The pilgrimage of prophets and poets
Withdrawn into a solitude of silence.
He thinks of Keats—the Elgin Marbles
Intensified and brilliant on the page.
He thinks of ages buried and forgotten,
Of epics and oracles and the mystical chantings
Of holy men in monastery alien to analyst and scholar.

He thinks of of Rilke's Book of Hours
And the last deep breath of Ezra in exile...

He watches as the black thick smoke of factories,
The certainties of Science, the vagaries of Chance
Try hopelessly to hide her. While the fragments
Of her form, shattered, distorted out of shape,
Like splinters of stars, are forever adrift in the darkness.

VII

The Marriage

Beyond the green sea
Where all memory had its origins,
Beyond the Green Rose & the Black Swan,
Shards of memory, splinters of selflessness.

The Man views the Woman
In the mirror of the reflected "I",

       Love springing like a fountain,

       Love vibrant as the air.

The light of illumination

Neither sun-sourced nor moon-reflected,

Quicker than Einstein,

Clear as the wind,

Burns with the beating heart,

Blazes in the blood of the Husband and the Bride.

SESTINA: Beata Mea Domina

> Fair shines the gilded aureole
> In which our highest painters place
> Some living woman's simple face.
> —Dante Gabriel Rossetti

FROM Beatrice to Guenevere we've seen you dressed;

Your face, those round full lips, the crispness of your hair...

How you must have lured them with those lips.

But the clearness of your eyes, with that vacant gaze

Tranquil as brook water, was, perhaps, the more telling

    fact,

The clincher, that is, which convinced them of your wonder.

Husband William must have beamed with suspicious wonder

When they came, poet-friends, to visit you, to gaze

With admiration at those eyes, those sweet ensanguined lips,

To capture in a word, a phrase, the essence of your hair,

Your face, that proud and stately manner in which you

    dressed.

Painters with their passion-strokes drew witness to that fact.

Like a mask of truth or a cloak of fictitious fact
We've seen you draped and veiled and dressed
In a fountain of color, enshrined in a statement of wonder.
We've seen the history of the past reveal itself in a gaze,
In the way your eyes had words and your lips
A wordless voice to match the language of your hair.

From your swan-like neck to the fullness of your hair,
We've seen you—sad and pensive like some old forgotten
      fact,
Enshrined within a temple of intoxicating wonder.
We've learned to separate the nude from the artist fully
      dressed,
To distinguish from the taste the vintage of your lips.
You've kept the beauty of the past secure within a gaze.

What dark foreboding spell lurks behind that gaze?
What truth is hid inside you, what sense of wonder

Compels our eyes to question both reason and fact
As if truth had design, to be polished and dressed
In a body-like fashion, to be woven like hair
In a maze of flesh, in the texture of lips?

With a madness for taste you've drawn us to your lips
Kiss-shaped and solemn like a swollen heart or a gaze
At some strange forbidden pleasure usurping vision and
    fact.
How you torture us with hunger, excite us with wonder
When the light upon your skin throws ripples through
    your hair.
How the light sustains the beauty that through your eyes is
    dressed.

MADRIGALS & MOTETS

Introduction

POETRY: what fools we are

to think anyone has need for such unessential

elements of language.

To observe and ponder the ivory of your hands,

the wordless dance of the stars,

the silence of your silken hair

and the air of fragrance

that accompanies the gift of all your kisses.

What fools! What wonderful magicians!

I

TEARS that stain the sight of vision
Sorrow has fed and parting has made,
Lightly, go lightly, O my lady
Leave these eyes and ascend up to heaven:
Nothing is delivered when nothing is braved.

Love that has died, though brief was its shining,
Sweet is the memory and sweet is its grace,
Lightly, go lightly, O my lady
Sooths the heart with acceptance when finding
Nothing is delivered when nothing is braved.

Lightly, go lightly, O my lady,
Night flies the sunrise and dies the old day!

II

MY LOVE:

I love you without reason or prayer,

Without any sensibility proper or sacred.

I love you crudely and crass,

I drool at the very mention of your name.

I love you till all the cows come home

Or the chickens come back to roost.

I love you without doubt or reservation.

I love you without shame or consternation.

The mere mention of your name

Sends me to strange exotic places.

III

LATE in the day
   The sea light quivers,
Eventide stirs
   The moon's face on water.
A sandpiper scurries
   On the moon-beaded sand
Like pearls on the wrist
   Of a woman's white hand.
A man holds a woman,
   Hearts pounding and glad,
The heat from their bodies
   Casts a glow on the glass.
The heat from their bodies
   And the moans from their lips
Melts the moon on the water
   In a total eclipse.

IV

BEAUTY runs rich in your deep brown bewildered eyes,
Groves of trees stand silently in your shadow.
A bed of white roses once covered your thighs
On the legs that I once called my pillow.

O rare is the wonder that sparkles inside
The house where our bodies kept singing,
And rare was the music that followed our song
Like the voice of the air in the evening.

O rivers of magic run swift in your eyes,
In an ocean of dreams your body shimmers.
Your lips have the smoothness their texture implies
When I am lured by the strength of your fingers.

O beauty flows swift through your circle-soft eyes

Dipped in an ether of loveliness.

My praise would turn false and my judgment unwise

If ever my love should prove faithless.

V

OF your amorous ways,
Will you yet spare me?
Prick-pressing flesh
Weary and wane.

From the sweat of your limbs
I slide and am carried
Inside and out
Till my body is drained.

Inside and out,
Above and below me,
You move like a minnow
Hooked in a lake.

You wriggle and whimper,
You worry and chide me
Should the rod of my reel
Ever go slake.

    She answers:

    Be careful, my love,
    How you mock me or goad me
    Or make light of my treasures
    You so willingly take.

    Take heed, if you value
    What I've snared in my belly
    Should the rod of your reel
    Bend over and brake!

VI

LILACS in the morning
Scent a fine perfume
When my lady goes out walking
The buds burst out in bloom

From sun into sunset
I've wandered and watched you

When my lady glides in motion
Upon the slippery air,
Her hair is like the ocean
Reflected in a mirror

Ring ring the bells
Of heaven to hill

Her hair and the air that follows,

Her eyes and her face so serene,
Her breasts like the down of a swallow
Her smile and the style of a dream

From sun into sunset
I've wandered and watched you.

Ring ring the bells
Of heaven to hill.

The light from the skies
Enshrines and surrounds you.
Let the light of your passion
Cover me still.

VII

WE breathe flowers you and I

We kiss the night with lips of sky.

With little silver cups asparkle in our hands,

We drink from the blood of God, the blood of Man.

We feed on star-milk you and I

We quench our thirst for love with light

Into a wondrous ocean of always our minutes dive and swim

Encircled by a womb of light half-lit and partly dim

O we challenge heaven you and I

By the music in our hearts, the wind in our eyes

Like the gladness of the gull our holy spirits sing

In a glimpse of eternal light, the quiet song of spring

O we challenge the heavens you and I

Though the truth of light will never say why

For the words of a rainbow are elusive and fade

Like the ghost of a swan on a river of jade

VIII

O THE stain won't come off

Where last I first touched you

O the touch is as sacred as ever

O the smell is still sweet

Where, trembling, our bodies grew

Like stems in the heat of hot weather

O pure is the stain

O warm the strange wonder

O fresh the sweet smell of young summers

O the stain won't come off

Where last I first kissed you

O the taste is as sacred as ever

IX

THERE are lots of bright flowers

In our morning

Sea-birds sing the sky to wakefulness

Where we dream

The great green hills are endless

In the distance

The earth wears a garment made

Of light and yellow leaves

There are warm and tender moments

In our morning

Your hair moves so graceful

Like the sea

The wind blows hard and forceful

Against the window

My sheets rest so peaceful

At your knees

X

I HAVE known many women

In my lifetime

Some as fair as a fountain,

Some as a dark as the night.

I have played their names

On the strings of my memories,

I have seen their faces

In the mountains and the skies.

TWO CHRISTMAS BALLADS
FOR GUITAR & KEYBOARD

I.   A Christmas Lullaby

II.   Winter Solstice

LEAD SHEET **CHRISTMAS LULLABY** J. R. PHILLIPS

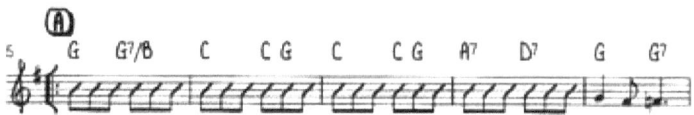

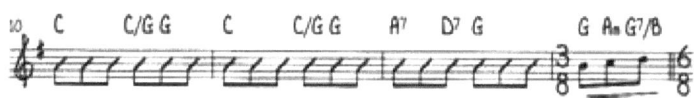

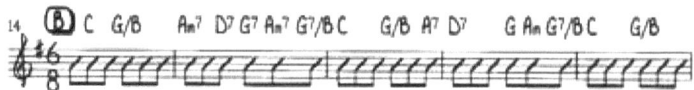

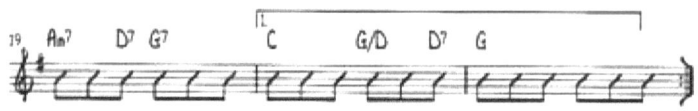

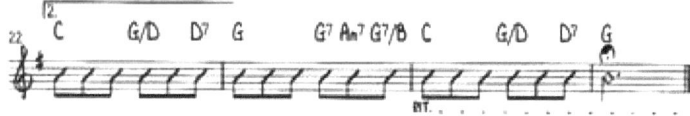

I. A Christmas Lullaby

In the windows of night
All the little babes are sleeping
And the snow keeps falling softly
On the little village town
I can see in your eyes
All those silver bells of Christmas
And the holly wreaths that hang so high
From the little chapel walls

—chorus –

Sing silent snow on the rooftops tonight
Sing through the air and the treetops so high
Praise to the earth and the heavens above
Cover and comfort with love
Cover and comfort with love

O be still silent night, be merciful and merry

Let the spirit of the season

Light a pathway to the stars

Shine with hope, shine with love

Shine above the burning ember

From the chimney tops and the bakery shops

Of the little village town

—repeat chorus –

II. Winter Solstice

Winter solstice in the evening
Christmas bells are ringing near
Stars are shining, lights are twinkling
Winter solstice in the air

—chorus—

Ringing bells across the city
Ringing bells of Christmas cheer
Ring forever in the country
Ring out loud throughout the year

All the streetlights of the city
Flash and flicker with great care
All the hilltops shine so pretty
Winter solstice in the air

—chorus—

Ringing bells across the city
Ringing bells of Christmas cheer
Ring forever in the country
Ring out loud throughout the year

Wake up darling, see the morning
Sunlight dancing in your hair
Snowfall melting on the window
Winter solstice in the air

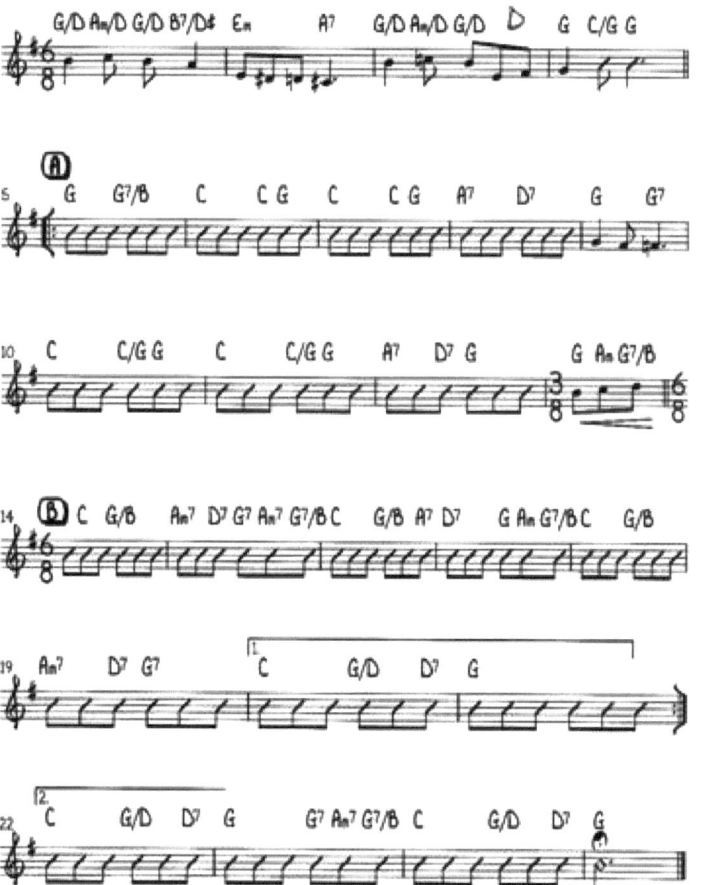

J.R. PHILLIPS— resides in Los Angeles, California. A graduate of California State University, Northridge where he studied writing under the guidance and encouragement of renown California poet, Ann Stanford, he is the father of three children and makes his home in the San Fernando Valley. He received an MFA in Creative Writing from Antioch University.

www.ingramcontent.com/pod-product-compliance
Lightning Source LLC
Chambersburg PA
CBHW041617220426
43671CB00004B/47